Barbara Susan Williams

Jacki
H

CW00405877

Chasing the Dragon by Jackie Pullinger with Andrew Quicke (Hodder & Stoughton) is acknowledged as a primary reference source.

Jackie Pullinger of Hong Kong

Facing the Darkness

Joan Clifford

Marshall Pickering

Marshall Morgan and Scott
Marshall Pickering
3 Beggarwood Lane, Basingstoke, Hants RG23 7LP, UK

Copyright © 1988 Joan Clifford
First published in 1988 by Marshall Morgan and Scott
Publications Ltd
Part of the Marshall Pickering Holdings Group
A subsidiary of the Zondervan Corporation

All rights reserved. No part of this publication may be
reproduced, stored in a retrieval system, or transmitted, in any
form or by any means, electronic, mechanical, photocopying,
recording or otherwise, without the prior permission in writing,
of the publisher.

ISBN: 0 551 01644 2

Text set in Baskerville by Brian Robinson, Buckingham
Printed in Great Britain by Cox and Wyman, Reading

Contents

For Marian Dawson

1

Hurry! Hurry! Hurry!

In the midst of the dusty West End streets of Britain's capital city, hundreds of young people are pressing forward, hurrying along, their faces bright and eager. Teenagers and young adults, they chatter and exchange smiling greetings as they swing along, but they do not stop.

What's the hurry? What are they making for? Is it a pop concert or an exciting demo? Are they marching with banners or waving flags? Are they going to welcome a sporting hero? No – it is Sunday evening – and they are going to church . . . .

A small notice on a board is the reason for this influx of people, young and more mature. One name on the board has magnetised them and urges them on. Oyez! If you don't come now, you may not get in.

Not find room in church! Can this be possible? Yes, it is and so it turns out. Many people cannot find seating in the large church and have to scurry downstairs to the crypt, where they can take part in the service by means of closed-circuit television. Every seat is taken and some late-comers have to stand at the back or sit on the floor. There is an air of expectancy, enhanced as eventually the vicar, attired in summer shirt-sleeves, comes in, followed by a group of young men and women.

Several Chinese stand out in the group, black-haired youngsters with guitars. There are one or two Europeans and there is one young woman, slightly older than the others. She is an attractive, youthful-looking woman, in a flowered dress, with shoulder-length brown hair falling round a vivacious fine-featured face. This group and especially the young woman, is the reason for the full church and the air of anticipation. She is Jackie Pullinger of Hong Kong, making the last public appearance of her British tour. She is the one they have come to see and hear.

A strange sort of fame accrues to Jackie. Who is she? She is not rich, or a political figure; not a pop star or a media figure – certainly not by her own wish. Some have called her a 'self-styled missionary' but no missionary society sent her to Hong Kong, no particular church owns her allegiance. She has had no special training. Yet she is famous all the same; famous for telling and showing the love of Jesus to the people of Hong Kong, particularly in the notorious Walled City. Famous for demonstrating that love and for sticking at it, year in and year out: she is 'Poon Siu Jeh' – 'Pullinger' – to the Hong Kong people and to many others; she is respected, admired and, above all, loved.

Prayers are said, simple hymns are sung – 'Jesus loves me' is the theme. Some people stand as they sing, some sit, some sway with emotion. In the crypt, a woman comfortably feeds a baby.

At last, Jackie stands up. She holds her heavy, well-worn Bible. She has a bright face. She speaks with confidence, but she is not excitable. She is introducing a young Chinese man who will give his witness. He is tall, well-built and good-looking, in a sparkling white shirt. His English is halting and he is under some emotion. It turns out that he has had little education of any kind, so his address in our language is even more amazing. He gives an unanswerable testimony of his experience of coming off the drug heroin. He confesses: 'I was an addict for more than ten years.' He is a living witness to 'new life in Jesus'.

But the congregation has been waiting to hear Jackie speak and now she draws everyone into the circle of her concern. You really could hear a pin drop. There is nothing 'preachy' about her but she is punchy and gritty in her words. She speaks of the special value to God of the poor and simple, the hopeless, and of how, when they find the Lord, they will form the main body of religious revival.

She speaks of the need to 'die daily', to ourselves and to the limitations we place on our own powers. She speaks of the miracles we should expect God to perform, of what can be achieved by spirit-filled lives. She also talks with seriousness of the need to be prepared for problems and even persecution which may confront young Chinese Christians in the future. But she speaks with confidence, without fear and her face is radiant.

Afterwards, many people come forward for prayer and blessing. An intimate tone enters the service; people who have to go get up and exit quietly. The atmosphere within the building is charged with power yet it is quiet and peaceful. Poon Siu Jeh has made her impact. She would say that she has been enabled to bring to many the impact of her Lord.

Some young people are deeply moved. Jackie is not one just for emotion. Her message is sharp and clear. She learned to deliver it in Hong Kong's Walled City, six thousand miles away . . .

2

To the City of Darkness

People in Hong Kong say: 'No sane person, European or Chinese, would go into the Walled City . . .' Known as the 'City of Darkness', it is a dingy, disgusting, lawless place, which the police seldom enter, and then only in groups. It is an area of the Far Eastern Crown Colony of Hong Kong which was never in British hands, but remained under Chinese administration until even that broke down. A sort of 'no-man's-land' shanty town developed and became a haven for vice of all kinds, a place to disappear into if you were running from the law. It is only six acres in size but houses thousands of Chinese, whose life-style is appalling.

There are rickety apartment blocks, lacking sanitation, with electricity tapped from the public supply, evidenced by a tangle of overhead wires and cables. The smelly, slimy, narrow alleyways and the disgusting so-called 'public toilets' are scarcely believable. Rats scurry past. As no-one is responsible for this awful place, hardly anything is improved. And the whole squalid area is under the flightpath of Kai Tak airport, with the thunder of jets day and night.

In this place, people are born and try to live. Many are criminals, many are young, young without hope. Illegal gambling dens, drug dens and prostitution houses abound. It is hard to live in the Walled City and keep self-respect.

Yet Jackie Pullinger has been going back and forth into this place of darkness and has even made it a home, on and off for twenty years. Its people are close to her heart, many of them her friends, even her 'family'.

But the Walled City would have seemed like a horrible nightmare to the young woman, scarcely more than a girl, who dreamed twenty years ago of being a missionary. An amazing journey took her from a comfortable middle-class home to a little primary school run by 'Auntie' Donnithorne in Hong Kong's 'place of darkness'.

*   *   *   *   *   *

Jackie was born in the English Home Counties, a twin and one of four girls – a bit of a disappointment to the father who had hoped for a boy. But what he did get were four tomboys who grew up loving sports – running, climbing, cycling, and knowledge-ably watching rugger. Theirs was a happy, lively home and the girls went to Sunday School. Whilst still a child, Jackie was impressed by the visit of a missionary to her church and thought missionary work a romantic idea, which never left her. She was unwise enough to mention this to other people who never let her forget it and were apt to remind her of it when she had done anything amiss. 'Don't forget you're going to be a missionary' they would stress nastily.

Jackie was a normal girl, enjoying life. But God, even from her childhood, had been real to her and when, a few years later, the girls in her form were confirmed as communicant members of the Church of England, she was happy to be one of them. She found the church service, when the Bishop laid his hands on her head, meant a lot to her and she did feel a gladness and lightness in her heart. It was, of course, pleasant to have a special white dress and a special Confirmation tea-party, to which relatives and godparents came. Everything was 'special'. Jackie made an inward dedication of her life to God.

As she grew up, life opened out and was full and exciting. School was stimulating and there was plenty of sport and friendship. Her love of music was fostered and in the holidays she worked in her father's factory. At Christmas, like other youngsters, she delivered mail for the Post Office. She was given the title 'Our Number One Post Girl' and even became Miss Croydon South in 1960. It was fun.

Jackie's musical talent led her to the Royal College of Music, where she studied piano and oboe. There was also now a lovely freedom to pursue other interests. Boy friends appeared on the scene, but nobody special. Jackie fell for the entire brass section at college and for a while followed them round like a pop groupie, happily sitting on their instrument cases in the train.

Every now and then she remembered her confirmation vows and her missionary dreams but life was now very full. The Christian Union put up their notices on the college board and Jackie felt she ought to go to their meetings but was frankly not attracted by the look of the members. Also, she was not sure she wanted to meet their challenges – just at the moment.

Then, by chance, an old school friend met on the train invited her to a coffee meeting at a London flat, to hear a special speaker who would talk about the Bible. Although not very keen, Jackie agreed to go. There she found seemingly ordinary and normal people, not upsettingly pious, but committed Christians. When they talked about God and Jesus, she did not feel in the least uncomfortable. In that little flat, she knew positively that she had to accept the Christian faith at a deeper level. 'I was converted', she says.

Changes came about in her life, not always in accordance with her wishes. She agreed to play the piano at a Christian Youth Squash one Saturday afternoon, instead of going to the Rugby International at Twickenham. Previously, she would have considered this a big sacrifice, but somewhat to her surprise she actually enjoyed herself.

But still she did not feel she had made any purposeful decision about the way her life should go. Having taken her music degree, she was teaching music and enjoying her work, but when she asked people, 'What shall I do with my life?', they were not a lot of help, usually suggesting 'Why don't you pray about it?', which she continually did. There seemed to be no clear answer.

One night she had a vivid dream, in which her family seemed to be poring over a large map, on which a pink-coloured area stood out. In the dream, Jackie bent over and read the name 'Hong Kong'.

When she awoke in the morning, the dream was recalled and still vivid. Hong Kong! Was that to be her true destination? Jackie found herself writing to the Hong Kong government asking if any music teaching posts were available and being disappointed at the answer 'no'. Then she wrote to various missionary societies, asking if they could use a music teacher in their schools, for she wanted to offer her own particular talents to God. The answers were not encouraging. They would have grabbed at a Maths or English teacher, but music was a luxury for mission schools. In any case, she was not old enough.

'We don't consider appointing anyone younger than twenty-five' they wrote. It seemed so final, and Jackie was depressed, sure than her dream had been a real sign.

A little later she visited another house-group of young Christians and there a great truth hit her. She seemed to hear a a quiet voice saying: 'Go, trust me and I will lead you . . .'

Somehow, though she was not really any further forward, Jackie felt reassured that some definite lead would soon be given her. She felt this so strongly that she gave in her notice at school and decided not to teach there any more after the summer term. She would be free and ready when the call came. This was a puzzle to her family.

Still nothing happened. Then Jackie thought of someone she could talk things over with, someone young enough to understand yet older than her and more experienced. So she went to see the Rev. Richard Thomson, then vicar of Shoreditch, in whose parish she would sometimes help. He was just the person to advise her at this time, since he had recently taken over a huge and worrying vicarage. Unsure whether he could cope, he then decided to act on faith and go ahead. To his joy, within six months, his vicarage was fully furnished and full of students. From his own experience, he felt confident to advise Jackie to take a bold step, one that other people at the time called 'irresponsible'. He suggested to her that if she felt God was calling her and had tried all the conventional ways of getting an answer, she should simply leave home, and set out for the Far East.

As he looked at this attractive young woman, full of personality, highly talented and with her strong Christian faith, he felt it was right to encourage her to throw herself upon God and go out in faith, in a scriptural way, like Abraham, and like many since then.

'Get a ticket and go' was the sum of his advice.

So Jackie did. Trusting Richard's advice and her own new-found confidence, she very soon found a ship going from France to Japan and in a short time embarked. On the boat train beforehand, she had said a muted goodbye to her parents and to Richard, who ran up the platform shouting 'Praise the Lord!', startling the onlookers. Jackie was not happy to be leaving her family, but she knew she had to go.

In due time, after a sea voyage in which she had plenty of hours to think about what she was doing, Jackie found herself in the harbour at Hong Kong, facing the Immigration Officer. She had arrived. A new life was about to begin.

3

Learning the way round

The Immigration Officer who had boarded Jackie's ship was not at all pleased to see her. He studied her papers and stared at this lone girl. He began a series of probing questions – 'Why had she come to the colony?' 'Where was she going to live?' 'How was she going to support herself?' 'How much money had she?' 'Who did she know in Hong Kong?'

None of the answers seemed to satisfy him; he shook his head. The idea of a young lady coming to the colony to tell people about the love of Jesus did not seem to appeal to him at all.

Jackie began to feel it likely that she would be bundled back to Britain and would never set foot in Hong Kong. Finally, in desperation, she mentioned a family acquaintance, a godson of her Mother's. 'He's a policeman here' she said hopefully.

This did the trick. The Officer's face cleared and he shrugged his shoulders. He had thought Jackie might be a good-time girl of bad morals looking for well-off American troops who were then being sent to HK for 'rest and recreation' away from the Vietnam war. In such a crowded territory, full of refugees, every would-be entrant had to be thoroughly interrogated. However, if she knew a policeman – she must be all right.

'Try to get a job quickly' he advised – 'your cash won't go far here!' He was right. It has been said of Hong Kong that the 'smell of money' is in the air. It is the place for making money and spending it. Jackie had only six English pounds which, in Hong Kong dollars, would not go far. But she was not worried. God had led her safely thus far and she was sure He would go on leading and supporting.

At last she was off the ship and had set foot in Hong Kong, called romantically the 'Pearl of the Orient'. Europeans first visiting here undergo 'culture shock', the feeling you get when you go somewhere very different. Jackie now knew this feeling. She took a few minutes to stand outside the ocean terminal in the brilliant sunshine, to look around, to listen and to savour the unfamiliar scents. Sight, sound and smell in Hong Kong assails you, you cannot escape it. The great harbour was alive with craft – imposing liners, gaily-coloured lighters, little bobbing fishing sampans and scurrying wallah-wallahs, a kind of water-taxi. Her eyes caught the elaborately-decorated floating 'fish restaurants' in the bay. Ferry boats plied busily across the waters, for Hong Kong consists of two hundred and thirty-six islands, some quite big, some tiny, all at the toe of great China. Along the waterside were the famous Chinese junks, with their red sails, which brought food to HK from mainland China.

As she lifted her eyes and looked across the bay, Jackie saw the go-downs – warehouses – and rising high like a hilly New York, the shining skyscraper blocks of modern buildings, apartments and offices. These were all on Hong Kong Island. She turned round; she was on the edge of Kowloon, the

19

peninsula crammed with Chinese. Looking beyond, twenty miles away, she saw the Hills of the Nine Dragons shimmering in the sunlight. Behind these was the huge nation of Chairman Mao's China.

Jackie was used to the sounds of a great city like London, but she was staggered by the burst of noise that assailed her eardrums. So many people! Such shouting and yelling! To the European ear, the Cantonese speak harshly and in the hectic life of Hong Kong, quiet is hard to find – it has to be positively sought. Everywhere Jackie felt the throb and thrust of the vast money-making centre.

Chinese people filled the streets and took little notice of Europeans, whom they think of still as 'gweilos' (foreign devils). Wealthy tourists sauntered by, peering into shops and enjoying the variety of fine goods.

Strange scents met Jackie's nostrils. As she moved along the crowded streets, full of cars, bikes and rushing pedestrians, her eyes caught the garish signs of the shops, in Chinese characters, hanging from the doorways. She smelt unusual odours that she would soon learn to recognise. These were even more pungent when she came to a market, where strange meats, fish, herbs, spices, vegetables and fruit were piled in abundance. It was all rather startling. And everywhere, the vast concourse of Chinese humanity, bright-eyed, black-haired and lively.

Jackie pulled herself together. She must find temporary lodging and work. 'Probably the best place to start is at a church' she thought. Before long she met Mrs Donnithorne, known as 'Auntie', who ran a nursery school and house church in the Walled City. It was Auntie Donnithorne who persuaded

20

Jackie to follow her into the Walled City – Hak Nam – 'place of darkness'.

It literally was dark in there, for the roofs of the rickety dwellings almost met overhead. Getting into the place was a puzzle, it was hidden from everyday Hong Kong. Auntie knew how to slip in between two shops, through a narrow gap. The contrast was painful – the sunshine, smart hotels and gleaming cars were left behind: in the Walled City it was gloomy and smelly. Jackie followed Auntie, who sped through the dingy alleyways and passages. It was rather, thought Jackie, like being in an under-ground tunnel. She was conscious of the rubbish, damp and filth that squelched beneath their feet as they trod the rotten duckboards that made up the 'pavement'. Jackie was conscious of a great deal of spitting, which has never offended Chinese people as much as it does Europeans. Auntie Donnithorne talked all the time, trying to explain the sights and sounds as they passed. It was almost too much to take in.

Some dwellers there did have proper business activities but of a limited and boring nature, like toiling in tiny dark workrooms making plastic flowers. It seemed there was no trade union to protect them and Sunday was no day of rest here. Children seemed to be working everywhere, like little slaves.

Many of the occupants of the Walled City lived on the edge of crime, if not actively engaged in it. Jackie, like most middle class English girls, had heard and read of these things. Now she was plunged into a scene where evil living was a fact of life and touched the lives of many young people. Boys and girls and little children were fixed into lives

21

of degradation, caught up in crime, in vicious behaviour, in a hopeless circle from which it seemed they could not escape.

Frail, elderly women shuffled by, bent and worn before their time; boys with the faces of little old men peered out and the dark listless eyes of little girl prostitutes looked at Jackie. She did not know what to think, except that it was clear that the love of Jesus had not penetrated here.

In this awful place, courageous Auntie Donnithorne had set up her small school and, on Sundays, a simple house church. Without really knowing what she was doing, Jackie agreed to teach singing, percussion band and English language on three afternoons each week. The music part turned out to be fine but the English teaching was hopeless. Jackie, without any Chinese language, and the children with a new and unexpected freedom from discipline, got nowhere. On Sunday nights, Jackie pedalled furiously at an old harmonium to accompany simple hymns. Some old Chinese ladies came, but they were more keen to learn a little English than anything about the Christian God.

The Chinese language is very difficult for outsiders to master. It has no alphabet but is formed by a series of characters, which have to be learned. Jackie knew that if she was going to get anywhere, she had got to beat this hard new tongue. Before long she had learned to say 'Hallo', 'How are you?', 'Where is . . .' and most important of all – 'Yeh sou ngoi nei' – Jesus loves you. It took Jackie five years to speak Chinese well and in this time she herself was given a Chinese name, meaning 'Pullinger', her surname. She came to be known as 'Miss Poon' or 'Poon Siu Jeh'. She was on her way to becoming 'one of them', but it was a hard road before she was really accepted.

Jackie found a job teaching in a well-run primary school in Hong Kong in the mornings and in the afternoon travelled the considerable journey to the Walled City. She began to feel that there ought to be somewhere where young teenage boys particularly could meet together in wholesome circumstances; if they had nothing to do, they soon got into trouble. Few in the Walled City had much education and they had not much to offer employers. But it was getting to know Chan Wo Sai that gave her the final push. This lad was an unpleasant teenager with a miserable background and was always in trouble. At this time, in 1967, there were riots in the colony, but Jackie did not then know much about the political life of the territory. She did discover that ignorant boys were being paid to throw stones and cause problems. They needed somewhere to work off their high spirits. A youth club must be the answer! 'Some fine people will come over from the Island to help me', thought Jackie. She had visions of a well-run, flourishing club with good support and marvellous programmes and everyone in it behaving well and becoming model citizens and young Christians.

The club started in a bare room borrowed from the school. No European would have thought it much of a place, nor indeed any of the Chinese outside the Walled City. Jackie could still speak only a few Chinese sentences and she had only one helper, Gordon, but they were in business. The club was called 'The Well' and its bare brightness was at least in contrast to the dingy streets and alleys outside. Gordon helped to arrange football, table tennis and darts and to make up parties to go roller skating, boating and camping. It was all basic, but soon The Well was full of young teenagers. They enjoyed the Club, having somewhere to meet, and having fun, but they were not at all keen on what they called 'the Jesus bit'. To them, anything to do with Christianity meant 'don't do this or that' and was very middle-class and respectable, which they knew well they were not.

Some of them were most unappealing, many had criminal connections, but Jackie grew fond of them and loved to see them happy, their dark eyes and white teeth shining.

Jackie could see that there were great gaps between the well-fed orderly Christians in the Hong Kong churches and the raffish boys and girls of the Walled City. She did not feel that the established churches were able or indeed very keen to help; certainly they were not being very successful.

She did not feel she was very successful either. Her lack of Chinese was frustrating; she saw that she needed to show her Christian caring through action. She began to do practical things for the boys, like going with them to job interviews, or helping them to get school places. She began to visit their awful homes to see what could be done.

For their part, the youngsters played her up a good deal. They were convinced she was a rich westerner and could give them money. They tried to get all sorts of things out of her. She had to make them understand that she herself had very little of this world's goods – she had not come out to Hong Kong to make money. This did not please them and they scarcely believed it.

'I'm not doing much for God in this place'

thought Jackie. She kept speaking and preaching but no one seemed to care. Deeply disappointed, she knelt down and prayed for new power. At least, she thought, the youngsters of the Walled City had now grasped the fact that she intended to stay with them and was not a 'fly by night evangelist'. They had met some who had come, uttered Bible phrases and then taken the next plane and left. At least she was here to stay. And, despite everything, she felt strangely content.

4

Friendship and Renewal

Of course Jackie found odd snatches of time in which to enjoy herself. Being young herself, she was full of wonder and interest at all around her and ready for adventure. Beauty and excitement abound in Hong Kong and the surrounding islands. She could not be parted from her love of music and found companionship and joy in playing her oboe in an orchestra of high standard. She began to realise how much of interest the colony held away from the razzamatazz of the business, shopping and tourist areas.

About seventy percent of Hong Kong is countryside and great natural beauty exists in the country parks, where fine trees, plants, birds and over two hundred kinds of large butterflies can be seen. Scenically, Hong Kong has much to offer; a landscape rising from sandy beaches and rocky foreshores, great for bathing, to heights of almost a thousand metres. In the Lion Rock country park you can tackle hazardous climbs.

Visits to the islands are fascinating too. On Cheung Chau you might see a Buddhist funeral, with the mourners wearing white garments like white coal sacks. On Lantau you can visit the colourful Buddhist temples and see the monks in their saffron robes. By contrast, you can know the peace and quiet of the Christian trappist monastery and drink a refreshing glass of milk from their herd of cows – a pleasant novelty in Hong Kong where fresh milk is practically unknown.

Jackie made friends easily by her outgoing, cheerful nature. She was beginning to understand the Chinese character, which she did not find at all 'inscrutable'. She began to appreciate the Chinese love of jokes and puns and to enter into their age-old culture. And of course she made European friends, especially among the young people from various countries who were working their way round the world and staying in Hong Kong for just a while. Some became her helpers at The Well.

Among church people, though they welcomed her, Jackie found some reserve. The older, rather traditionally-trained missionaries, did not seem to be always on her wave-length. She accepted that she must seem rather unusual to them, coming to the colony on her own, without any formal missionary training, and working in her own individual way, without any great missionary society to support her. But Jackie found it hard to believe in their assertion that a kind of spiritual cloud hung over China and Hong Kong and that this was not yet ready to be dissipated. Surely this could not be true!

They also had rather rigid, set patterns of behaviour that they thought suitable for their position which made Jackie restless. She found their warnings and suggestions irksome and not useful. She did not want to be bothered with little habits and customs that seemed to her fussy and pointless.

The church members that she met also seemed to be set apart from the young people of the Walled City. 'The churches are full of good people,' she thought, 'but the streets are full of poor people who need Jesus even more.' It seemed to be a case of the 'twain never meeting'. A great gap existed.

Jackie was feeling rather disappointed; it was crisis time in her life, when a great change occurred. It began at a service where she was impressed by a young Chinese couple who were the lay preachers in charge. They affected her by their certainty and their loving aura. Afterwards, she hurried up to talk to them. They said bluntly, 'You have not got the Holy Spirit'. This rather annoyed her. She was sure she did have, else why had she come all this way from England? Rather unwillingly she agreed to go to their flat and talk further. 'You will know when you have the Spirit' they said emphatically, 'and you will receive other gifts that God has promised.'

Jackie was puzzled but in due course she climbed the stairs to their typically modest flat. In their living room, they laid their hands upon her head and prayed to God that she should receive the gift of the spirit. They were sure this would first show itself in the power to 'speak in tongues'. This is a special way of praying, in which people speak in a strange, sweet-sounding language when they talk to God; when interpreted, a spiritual message is given. It is a kind of heavenly language.

Jackie knew that the scriptures do talk about spiritual gifts, of certain unusual powers given to people and was reminded of some words of the Apostle Paul in his first letter to the church in Corinth. Here he talks about this gift of heavenly utterance which, he says, is the speaking of secret truths by the power of the Holy Spirit. St Paul agrees that this speech is mainly understood by the person using it and perhaps one or two others who can discern its meaning and can pass this on. She decided it was a bit of a mystery, which indeed it is, and wondered if it would apply to her.

Her Chinese friends were upset that, at first, nothing remarkable seemed to have happened. 'Now you speak!' they urged. Jackie was getting hot and rather cross. She finally decided it was all rather embarrassing and opened her mouth to say 'Help me, please, God' when it happened and she found herself praying in this new way, strange and beautiful words pouring from her. She no longer cared if anybody heard and she found a new freedom and abandon in praying in this way. Her Chinese friends were delighted and promised that other spiritual gifts were sure to appear. Jackie felt a bit shaken; she was not sure that she was ready for anything else to happen. So she picked up her bag and said goodbye and hurried home.

She talked to people around the colony about this new experience but did not get a lot of help. She decided not to worry about using this new prayer-language. Did it have much point?

About a year passed, when she met a family who were to make the utmost difference to her life and service. They were Americans, Jean and Rick Stone Willans, travelling with their daughter and a friend. They had come on a preaching and prayer mission to Hong Kong, though as it happened they stayed on. They advertised that they would be holding 'meetings', and that these would be 'charismatic'. This meant that they expected gifts of the Holy Spirit to be received at these gatherings. *Charisma* is a Greek word meaning 'gifts of grace'.

Jackie thought it rather presumptuous to come to a place in this way, when it was already well

29

supplied with churches and prayer groups and visiting missions. But in spite of herself, she was interested at the thought of the special nature of the meetings, so she went along and joined a crowd in the hall. She found the Willans couple most attractive and their talk persuasive and appealing. They were also forthright.

After their meeting, Jackie went up to chat and Jean at once asked Jackie if she 'spoke in tongues'. Jackie murmured that she had not found this very useful. Jean was not impressed. 'It's a holy gift, Jackie, and not to use it is very bad manners! It's a present!' This rather startled Jackie, but she could not but be convinced by the shining sincerity of Jean and Rick. Soon the three of them were praying quietly in this new heavenly language and Jackie felt completely comfortable. She thought: 'All right, Lord – if you invented this, it must be a good gift. I'll go ahead in obedience. Lord, teach me how to pray.'

She would say now that you do not have to understand everything that is said in tongues – she feels that in this process God is sorting you out. 'God is not hurtful', she says, 'He only brings things up when they are going to be healed. In tongues, God is unwinding things for us. He made us and He knows us and He wants us to be whole.'

After this encounter with the Willans family, Jackie felt greatly relaxed and restful and renewed. And after leaving the gathering, she made up her mind to pray like this every day for fifteen minutes, whether she felt like it or not. She kept this promise. After a few weeks, she suddenly noticed something amazing in her life. People she talked to about Jesus suddenly believed and were quite changed. She thought – Has my Chinese marvellously improved? Have I stumbled on a splendid new way of putting my ideas forward? But no, she knew that she was doing and saying exactly the same as before. It must be she herself who was different. Now she was not fretting and worrying, but letting God speak through her. By being obedient to His Will, results were coming.

Now, when she told people what she had herself for so long believed – 'Yeh sou ngoi' – Jesus loves you – many took her words to be true and believed. She knew a new and glorious freedom and power. She had truly received a spiritual gift, that of being able to bring people to her Lord.

5

Helping the Triad boys

Crime in the Walled City was controlled by two gangs of Triads. These Triads, secret societies, had originally been groups of men who plotted to restore the ancient ruling house of China, the Ming dynasty. Later, they became mainly gangs of men and teenage boys who ran crime rackets and made a lot of money by this. They were feared in Hong Kong and were a menace to police and society.

In the Walled City, two main gangs ruled, each having jurisdiction on their own side of a dividing street. They were known as the 14K and the Ging Yu. They had secret silent 'watchers' who knew as soon as anyone entered the Walled City and who ran and reported to their boss. These Triads, rather like the Italian Mafia, considered themselves to be a sort of family. There were rituals when anyone joined – they had to take oaths, shed and drink blood, and adopt special signs and handshakes. Their oaths were severe and binding. If a boy became a Triad member, he was supposed to remain one for ever. You swore loyalty to your boss, who was known as 'Big Brother', or in Cantonese, your 'Dai Lo'. You became his 'Little Brother' or 'Sai Lo' and you were bound together for all time.

This made it very hard for anyone to break out of

the Triad society. They were a nasty lot, mixed up in all kinds of crime – opium dens, drug trafficking, gambling, blue films, prostitution, illegal dog restaurants and 'protection' rackets among shop-keepers.

There seemed to be only one redeeming feature – that the 'Big Brother' had responsibility for his underlings and if they got into trouble, and were imprisoned, they were 'looked after' in prison and food and probably drugs smuggled in to them. The Big Brothers were not keen on drugs for the Triad members themselves, for they knew that the taking of drugs made the sai los less useful and manageable.

Jackie was forced to realise the sinsister division of the Walled City into the territories of these gangs. She discovered that her Youth Club room, which she had opened in all innocence, was right in the middle of the 14K Triad area. Very sensibly, she familiarised herself with every exit from the Walled City, so that she could make a quick getaway if necessary.

She began to understand how difficult it was for young boys to keep out of the Triads, if they had unhelpful families, miserable homes, poor education and no one to help them on and up. Any lad wandering about the Walled City who had no gang allegiance would soon be in trouble.

Christopher, for example, a young teenager, was trapped by 14K gangsters in an alley from which he could not escape and since he did not belong to them, or indeed, since he was so young, to any gang, he was at once set upon and badly hurt. The 14K left him doubled up with pain; he limped off and would not go back to that patch.

When Jackie saw him, she felt quite sick. He had been attacked by Chinese kung-fu boxers and really injured. Triad gangs were loosely linked and could call out hundreds of supporters for a big fight if they felt it necessary.

Not surprisingly, Christopher agreed to be initiated into the 14K Triad so that he could at least walk somewhere in the Walled City without getting set upon. He hung his head when Jackie tried to talk him out of it. He tried to squeeze past her, but the big accordion she was carrying prevented this. Jackie made him listen to her – the last thing he wanted to do.

'Who does Jesus love – good people or bad?' asked Jackie.

'Good ones of course!' he replied.

'Wrong!' said Jackie. 'If He were alive here to-day, He'd be sitting here on an orange box talking to all you lot here, and worse ones than you.'

Christopher scarcely believed this. 'Why?' he asked, wonderingly.

'Because He loves you and came to save those that are lost and have done wrong.'

Jackie and Christopher sat down on the filthy roadside, the jets thundering overhead as they do all day. Here in this horrible place, Christopher came to see that he was important to Jesus. He shut his eyes and prayed quietly in his own stumbling manner, asking Jesus to help change his life and to start again. There, in that unpromising situation, he became a Christian.

Things would not be easy for him. It was hard enough in the Youth Club where the boys at least knew what the club stood for. He had to endure some jeers and taunts. Members thought that people like

Christopher, from rotten backgrounds, did not become Christians.

Harder still, he knew he had to face the Triad bosses and say that he had made up his mind not to go ahead with the initiation. He sent back the papers from the Triad he was supposed to study. Nobody could remember such a thing happening before. But he stood firm.

Jackie was overjoyed. She almost cried with joy. Christ was alive and working in Hong Kong as anywhere else. Those who looked for Him would not be sent away sad and empty.

A big change came over Christopher. He cut out gambling and paid more attention to his work at the factory, where he soon became a supervisor. He was a great help in the Youth Club and was seen at the Sunday services. He did not slide back.

The first fully-initiated gangster to become a Christian was Ah Ping. He was sixteen and in his own eyes a real man of the world. He had joined the Triads when only twelve and was already renowned as a street fighter, with his own sai los. At fourteen he had become financially supported by a young bar girl, who brought him money in exchange for the protection of his muscles. Yet he was not insensitive. One evening at the club he saw that Jackie was depressed.

He shook his head. 'You ought to go back to England' he advised. 'We're no good here; we take your money and lose the jobs you find us. We'll never change – why do you stick around?'

Jackie looked up at him and words came rolling out.

'I stick around because that's what Jesus did for me; He didn't wait until I became good . . . He died for me . . . this Jesus only ever did good things. He died for me. He was the Son of God. He died for you too.'

For a long while, Ah Ping said nothing. He looked genuinely puzzled. At last he said: 'No one could love us like that, we're really rotten. We fight and steal and rape and knife. Who could really love us?'

Jackie stood up. 'Jesus does,' she said. 'He doesn't love the awful things you do, but He loves you. It doesn't make sense, I agree, but it's true. You'll find it's true. He'll give you a new life if you just ask Him – make you clean – whole – help you to start again.'

Ah Ping stopped pretending to be a man of the world. He looked shattered. There on the Youth Club doorstep he sat down and told Jesus that he couldn't understand how anyone could love him like that, but he wanted that love for himself. Then and there he asked Jesus to forgive him, change him and make a new man of him.

After that he had many temptations and crises. He was one day attacked by wild Chiu Chow gangsters, big strong men. He was left with a gash in his back and a hole in his throat. His father sought help from the 14K Triad who sent him to a doctor. He could not speak for several weeks.

But he protested strongly when his brothers determined to seek revenge on the fighters. Knives and choppers were taken out of their secret caches. Ah Ping shook his head, waved his arms about and muttered through his injuries, 'No, no, not now – I'm a Christian – you must not fight back.'

All through that night prayers were said in the Youth Club room for the gang who had hurt him so. He also asked for healing and hands were laid on

36

him. By morning he was restored and to everyone's amazement, could now talk properly.

Ah Ping made a complete break with his former gang and everyone knew it. Many respected him. He was always bringing criminals to the Youth Club, scruffy, difficult lads. Some of the better brought up lads, students, could not cope with this and left. Jackie did not worry too much – she knew there were plenty of places in the Colony where nice guys could feel at home. Getting them all to work together would take some time. But she rejoiced over Ah Ping.

* * * * * *

Jackie was now used to being awakened at all hours by people seeking help, since her name was now well known and she was trusted. But she was not prepared for what she found when a call on the phone at five a.m. summoned her urgently to the Youth Club room from her Kowloon flat.

On reaching the club room, she saw the reason for the distressed cry that had brought her there. 'Someone's broken in!' she had been told. Someone certainly had and not primarily to steal. It was as though hatred was being shown to her and all that she stood for.

Equipment was broken. Benches, tennis tables and skateboards were smashed up and thrown about. Books had been ripped up, sewage deliberately smeared on the walls and floor. It was a disgusting sight.

It was tough even for Jackie, who had by now grown accustomed to the horrors of the Walled City. After four years of really trying to help these boys – how could this be the response? She felt resentful and was almost in tears. She did not want to turn the other cheek and forgive this mess.

But she remembered a Bible verse about praising God even in your troubles and one about blessing those who persecute you. Reluctantly, muttering under her breath, she blew her nose, wiped her face, got hot water and brushes and fiercely set about cleaning up the room. 'Praise God! Praise God!' she sobbed, banging away with the bamboo brushes and sloshing water about. When she had finished, she gathered up the ruined equipment and mechanically sorted out anything fit to be used again.

The next night, defiantly, she re-opened the Club. But she felt low and rather frightened. She feared rejection by the boys she had come to love and care about. She suddenly felt alone and vulnerable, just one English girl in a strange and weird situation. What was she really doing here?

Suddenly a Chinese youth she had never seen before, poked his head round the door and nodded at her coolly. 'Got any trouble? Just let me know.' He swaggered a little.

'Who are you?' asked Jackie.

'I'm Winson and Goko sent me.'

Wonder of wonders! Jackie had often heard of the so-called 'Great Goko', the mysterious leader of the whole Walled City Triad set-up. He really was 'Mr Big', controller of a vast crime empire. Goko had always refused to meet her. Why had he sent this Winson?

It turned out that Goko had instructed Winson to go along and guard Miss Poon's place and 'do' anybody who bothered her. Winson certainly looked capable of this and turned up every night at the same time and hung about outside the club. For some time he acted nonchalantly and would not come inside – after all, he was a very big Triad himself, the 14K fight-fixer. But one night, he accepted Jackie's invitation to 'come inside'. Here he told her about a 'friend' with an opium problem. Jackie, of course, soon recognised that Winson himself was the 'friend in trouble'. To their surprise, he joined in the club hymn sing-song, making a tuneless but joyful noise, then began to pray in Chinese in his own peculiar way. Then, to everyone's astonishment, he started to pray in the new heavenly language which Jackie used, but of which he had no previous knowledge. After a time he stopped and it was clear to all that he had been delivered from his drug addiction. A true miracle had taken place. Through prayer, he experienced a painless withdrawal from drugs. And he went back to Goko to say that he could no longer be a gang member.

Later Jackie heard that a discontented member, who wrongly blamed Jackie for some misfortune, had been the instigator of the attack on the Youth Club, gathering together friends who had no idea what it was all about, but were just a violent mob. When Goko had heard of this, he had sent Winson as a guard and ordered the offenders to go back to the Youth Club and behave.

They were hesitant. 'She won't have us back', they said.

'Oh yes she will' said Goko. 'Miss Poon is a Christian and she will forgive you and let you in again.'

It was to be a long time before Jackie and Goko met face to face and had a real confrontation, but at least, she reflected, Goko did know what a Christian was expected to do and be and that was something.

6

Free to Help

Jackie began to feel the many pressures on her. She was young and strong but by now she hardly ever knew a real night's sleep. She was always being awakened by knocking during the small hours – someone looking for 'Miss Poon'. The youngsters in the Walled City were mostly 'night birds' whose unsavoury and illegal activities took place very often while others slept. They were wide awake and often in trouble.

She was feeling the strain also of full and compressed days. By now she was teaching music in a select school for girls, where the standards were high and she did her job well. She was proud of her professional skills but good lesson preparation was essential. On top of this were many demands by people in genuine need. How could she cope with all of this? Nothing could be done properly if you were for ever yawning, tired out and not on top of things. Occasionally, being a normal and pretty young woman, Jackie thought of what the situation would be if she were married. Her sense of humour took over – how would a husband like it if you were for ever ringing up and saying 'Can't get home yet, darling, I've got to deal with an addict – just get on with the dinner!'

But it was not really a joke. Jackie felt she was being pulled apart. She also needed much more time to conquer the Chinese language, which is so difficult for foreigners. Without this, she knew she would be constantly frustrated and her mission hampered.

As was her practice, she turned to God in prayer about this problem. It was gradually borne in upon her that she had quite enough to do in serving other people without going to work at all! Yet how could this be? She was an honourable young woman and had to work to receive pay. She put all this before the Lord.

'Well, Lord, I haven't got enough time to help all these people while I have to go to work. You promised to provide daily bread. Is there a chance you will provide mine without my having to earn it, so that I can do more for you in the Walled City?' It seemed a bit of a cheek, but here she left it.

A few days later, a phone call from a friend came straight to the point. 'Jackie,' said the friend, 'when you leave St Stephen's, we will offer you some regular living expenses.'

Jackie gasped. 'How could you possibly know that I was thinking of resigning my job? I haven't talked to anyone about this, except in my prayers.'

'Oh,' replied the friend. 'It's obvious to us that you will just have to leave – the work is going so well and you are so busy, you just cannot go on disappearing each day to teach. Others can do that, not everyone can do the work here.'

Jackie wondered whether she should let her friends part with their money like this. She was hesitant, but the friend was determined, almost sharp. She told how she and her husband had prayed about this matter and had come to the same conclusion – Jackie must be released for Walled City work. She must have living money – there was only one solution. They had to help.

That November day, quite bright even in Hong

41

Kong, became even brighter. Jackie felt this must be an answer to her prayer and she must not turn away this offer. She had to work out her contract at school, it would not have been honourable to do otherwise; she would put in her resignation and leave the following summer.

'That's fine', said the friend. 'We won't have the money till then.'

For Jackie this was another turning point, the moment when she began to 'live by faith' as she put it. She believed that if God had so appointed things that, without her having spoken to anyone, friends were offering her a reliable and regular sum of money for her personal needs, she had no right to worry further. She would turn over her life to God in its entirety, without the harassment of trying to split herself into segments as she had been trying to do.

It has always been difficult for some people to understand or accept this new way of life that Jackie had embraced. Up to the time of the phone call, Jackie had never even heard the phrase 'living by faith', but she saw that it was the right and practical thing for her. And from then on, the wells of sufficiency never ran dry. Friends provided food and rent money, not only for Jackie herself but also for the growing number of unfortunates for whom she seemed to be responsible.

One visitor thought it all most peculiar. 'What do you do for money?' he asked. 'We pray for it and it comes' was all that Jackie could say. The visitor plainly thought this most unlikely.

At that moment, a knock on the door brought in an old man, whom Jackie had never seen before, holding an envelope marked simply 'Jackie Pullinger, Walled City'. Inside was an American one hundred dollar bill.

The name of the giver was unknown to Jackie. She brandished the note before the visitor's eyes. They both smiled. 'No more to be said' he agreed.

* * * * * *

Jackie wrote out her notice and gave it to the school authorities. It was a big step to take. No more personally earned money from her good professional qualifications; no more accumulating personal bank balance. But she believed that God had now graciously given her a special freedom to spend her days in His service in a special way. The favoured girls in her school had benefited from their music tuition; how much more did the deprived youngsters of the Walled City need her. They needed not merely her guitar and accordion, but much more the knowledge of the forgiving love of God in their lives. This could free them from their present miserable existence and give them new dignity and hope. Jackie knew what her priorities must be.

She had been given a new power through her rich prayer life. She had now been given time – all the time in the world. How would God use it?

Every so often she sent a message to the powerful gang leader Goko, he who had ordered the 'tin-man-toi' (watchman) to stand guard over the Youth Club. She found herself very curious about this figure and anxious to meet him. At last, she received a reply that he would talk to her. He chose for a rendezvous an expensive Chinese restaurant outside the Walled City where foreign food was served. Jackie felt some exitement; she had heard so many tales about Goko; how he himself did the planning of his vast vice empire but lay for hours in his den while young Triad 'brothers' fed him with opium.

He was angry when the brothers took heroin themselves, for they were then quite useless as fighters and workers but opium, at any rate for himself, he considered merely a long-established social custom. He was known to be scrupulous in his responsibility for his Triad members, in seeing to funerals and making payments to dependants. A colourful character, Jackie decided. Could they have anything to say to each other?

She entered the Fairy Restaurant, the only westerner, and sat down. At the appointed hour, Goko appeared in the doorway. Smartly suited as befitted his lifestyle, he was a person of obvious authority in his mid-thirties. He was tall and well-built for a Chinese man. He had been handsome in the oriental manner but his face was lined and his strong features already affected by years of dissipation. Like all addicts, his teeth were stained and rotten. Despite this, he had a smile of some charm and greeted Jackie courteously, ordering light refreshments for them.

Jackie had not met him to engage in social pleasantries. 'Don't be so polite' she said abruptly. 'We have nothing in common – why are you being so pleasant to me?' After a pause, Goko replied: 'I believe you do care about my brothers.' Jackie responded that she certainly did but she had the greatest wish in the world to get them away from him.

'I will give the addicts to you' said Goko grandly. 'I know you can get them off heroin.' Jackie saw through this. 'Oh no,' she replied, 'you only want this so they will do your horrible work better for you.

44

I want them to get off drugs to start a new life, away from you and your rackets.'

Goko considered this. Then he looked directly at her and said, 'OK, I will give up my right to any of them who want to follow your Jesus.'

Jackie could hardly believe her ears. She had been told ever since she came to Hong Kong – 'Once a Triad member, always a Triad member – you can never get free.' Yet here was Goko, making what was for him, an amazing offer.

With a sort of teasing smile he went on: 'I'll give you all the rotten brothers and keep the good ones for myself.'

Spiritedly, Jackie responded. 'That's fine. Jesus came for the rotten ones, anyhow.'

The exchange was over. Having made this strange pact, Goko stood up and bowed and left. Jackie sat there for a while, amazed. What would this lead to?

From then on, Goko sent heroin addicts from his Triad to Jackie for cure and made no further demands on her. Apparently the buzz was round the city, that he had heard of the cure of one hard case and had said: 'I'm watching to see what happens to Johnny. If he lasts five years drug-free, I might have to believe for myself.'

Amazing things were happening in the Walled City.

7

Chasing the Dragon

Drug problems in Hong Kong could not be ignored.
They were seen particularly in the Walled City.
Drugs are prescribed by doctors frequently for sick
people and often work wonders. But they have to be
controlled and patients watched very carefully to see
that they take only the amount of tablets or pills
advised by the doctor.

Illegal drug-taking, when people become
'hooked' on drugs – as indeed some are on
cigarettes, alcohol and gambling – is a terrible as
well as criminal procedure. The 'high' which the
takers promise themselves eventually leads to
distress; addiction requires satisfaction. Addicts
need money and often turn to robbery; the
addiction itself causes physical misery and mental
decay and sometimes leads to death. As one writer
has said of the drug opium, 'It makes hungry where
most it satisfied.' In other words, once you are
'hooked', you are dependent upon it. A person
continually taking heroin, for example, can become
hooked in a fortnight.

Opium is the dried juice from the seed pod of the
opium poppy. A plant bearing fragile flowers of red
and white, it thrives in hot climates. It has been used
as a pain-killer for centuries, but when smoked or

eaten illegally it saps energy and mental strength. The drug heroin is derived from opium.

Hong Kong has had drug problems for years – drugs were easy to obtain and cheap – and the Government has been well aware of this. There are thousands of addicts in the colony, though millions of dollars have been spent by the Government to try to stamp out the unlawful drug trade.

Chinese drug addicts are in the grip of either opium or heroin. It is not too hard to understand that the drugs may seem a dream-like relief to people whose whole lives are miserable, poor and perhaps hungry. Users become a pathetic sight; they do not eat regularly or cannot be bothered to wash. During Jackie's years in Hong Kong, she had been forced to see at first hand the dreadful effects of the drugs on the population. After a while she became really depressed. During her visits to the crowded, poor quarters of the territory it seemed that she could not look anywhere without her eyes falling on some wretched creature in the grip of 'the dragon'. She longed to help them, to set them free.

Travelling in a minibus one day, a teenager sat near her who was obviously a victim. He looked like a pathetic skeleton – thin, with huge eye-sockets and his skin was a nasty grey colour. She recognised him as a boy she had previously seen opening taxi doors at a large and fashionable tea-house. He did not look as though he would be able to manage even this soon.

A terrible anger rose in her at the drug-pushers, the criminals who set up the drug rackets, many living in the Walled City. She felt anger, and sadness too at the wasted, spoiled lives, the early deaths.

When she had first traversed the Walled City, in the company of Auntie Donnithorne, she had been ignorant and unable to identify the drug victims. Now she recognised them only too well.

One night, at her request, she steeled herself to enter a heroin den. She was taken to one by an acquaintance. She had seen pictures in old books about the Orient, of old-time dens, where pigtailed men lay on divans with long pipes in their mouths. Today's scene was just as weird and revolting to her. This dirty shed was known to the police. Presumably they kept an eye on it and had a slight control over it. There were about fifty people looking, as Jackie says, 'like effigies', mute, immobile, sunk in their degrading private world. They were slumped over long tables, ruled over by the host, the 'pahng-jue'. He it was who took the money and handed out the equipment – screws of toilet paper, tinfoil and cardboard funnels.

Jackie started when she saw that one drug-taker was just a teenager, unhealthy and waxen-looking, who lay in the arms of an even younger girl, who looked at him tenderly. Probably the girl had had to sell her body to support the drug habit of her boy friend. Jackie reflected that this was probably true of most of the younger men there – they had to get money somewhere and an obliging or even reluctant girl friend was the only alternative to robbery or pawning the family belongings.

The drug takers, in the modern way, engaged in the weird ritual known as 'chasing the dragon'. The drugs were prepared in such a manner that the fumes were inhaled by mouth from a pool of melted heroin wriggling and sliding across a base of silver foil – hence 'chasing the dragon'. To watch the taker's sucking movements was a sad and disgusting sight; it was all an ante-chamber to hell.

Jackie had now seen enough of drug victims to feel intense pity for them. She knew that if they underwent the Government withdrawal programme they would suffer horribly for three days – agonies of chills, fever, vomiting and stomach cramps. If they continued on their horrid way, subject to the rule of 'Miss White' (heroin white powder) their entire personalities would collapse.

But in spite of her distress, Jackie no longer felt totally desolate for she had seen young Winson, her guardian of the Youth Club, come off drugs gently and permanently, through praying in tongues. She now knew it could be done; the power of the Holy Spirit was more than equal to that of the terrible dragon – but the victim had first really to want to stop the habit. This was the trouble, they were often torn between self-disgust and the demonic pull of the drug.

8

Trial and error

Just outside the Walled City stood a steaming noodle
barrow. Late one evening, Jackie was standing
enjoying a bowl of noodles and some Won ton
dumplings after a busy day. She was asking around
about the chances of empty accommodation. She
had to find more space to give a home to her boys.

Helping the Triad boys to kick the drug habit was
one thing: helping them to develop a new style of life
was another. How could it be any good if the boys
went back to their old haunts and bad companions?
Temptation might well prove too strong.

Winson, for example, the club night watchman,
was still living in an opium den. It was no good
telling him to go elsewhere as he had nowhere else to
go.

Jackie's enquiries were overheard by a decently-
dressed Chinese lady who, seemingly miraculously,
offered straightaway the tenancy of a large derelict
building. Jackie went at once to see it. It was an
enormous place. As the woman admitted, it was in a
terrible condition – crumbling walls, holes
everywhere, no light or proper sanitation. But it was
roomy and available for a modest rent. Living room
is the most precious and scarce thing to find in
overcrowded Hong Kong.

Before Jackie could decide what was the most prudent way for a young, unmarried woman to operate this hostel, Winson had moved his few belongings in, followed at once by Ah Ping and Ah Keung, who were also homeless. They all pitched in to clean up the building and make it more of a home. They were not very skilful with tools but they ran about enthusiastically, banging and hammering and laughing. Jackie felt it must be right. When her friend Mary, who was going to share and help, first saw the house in Lung Kong Road, she burst into tears.

Even Jackie had some qualms. Perhaps she thought in passing of what her parents would have said about the place. Perhaps for a moment she had a mental picture of the neat modern home, should she have married, she would have had in England. But she shrugged off these thoughts. She saw the boys laughing and happy. 'It's all worthwhile' she told herself.

A bonus to the house was the flat roof, which became a pleasant roof-garden once the rusting bicycle frames and old bedsteads had been exchanged for flower tubs. It became a true home for the young converts who could not get their own accommodation since they had no proper job, no references and could pay no rent.

Jackie realised she had much to learn. At first she did far too much for the boys. She cleaned, cooked, fed them, washed clothes, found garments for them, found them simple work, found schools. In addition she was also going to the Walled City club each evening and visiting vice-haunts when the opportunity came to speak for Jesus. The house at Lung Kong road, now becoming known in the

51

neighbourhood, was constantly besieged by drug addicts, girls in moral danger, detectives seeking information and police with questions. It was a hectic time.

It dawned on Jackie that her charges were taking advantage of her and they they would never learn to stand on their own feet if she cossetted them as she was now doing. It was not easy getting them to take responsibility. 'Sometimes,' she said, 'I feel as though the boys are running me.' Being accepted as their friend, it was difficult for her to be also leader and disciplinarian.

She learned to lean upon and draw strength from her own friends. Jean and Rick Willans often opened their home to the boys, who loved going there – Jean and Rick were easy mixers in their company and had the knack of drawing the best from the boys. And no matter how the family grew in Lung Kong Road, the money to support them seemed to appear. It was truly amazing.

*　　*　　*　　*　　*　　*

Jackie found herself spending a lot of time at the police station and in the magistrate's court. People in trouble were always ringing her number and asking if Miss Poon could come and help. Such was now her reputation, they were convinced she would never refuse them. Walled City people had a deep distrust of the legal system and were not keen on giving evidence in court. Police and detectives had a difficult job in trying to deal with so many known criminals but it seemed to Jackie that Walled City boys were often arrested on flimsy 'evidence' and since they could not afford to pay for legal representation, they often pleaded guilty to things they had not done.

There was also some corruption among the police, certain of whom allowed drug-dens to remain open for 'kick-backs', whilst organising show-raids in the Walled City from time to time.

'It's very hard,' thought Jackie, 'for the boys to sort out the good guys from the bad!'

She determined to identify with the boys in their misery and to go with them when they needed support. This could be anytime. Walking one day in Kowloon with Ah Ping, he suddenly said 'I've got to the end of the street and haven't been arrested!' The boys grew cynical in their attitude to the law.

Jackie knew only too well what awful things the boys often did, but she objected to their being punished for something they had not done and constantly urged them: 'Just tell the truth.'

Johnny was one boy arrested and found guilty in a case where Jackie was certain he had done nothing illegal. The Police Inspector shrugged his shoulders. 'This is Hong Kong justice, Miss,' he said. 'Even if he hasn't done this one, he's done others. It's fair in the long run.'

Jackie shook her head and the tears came into her eyes. It was so unfair. The detectives obviously thought she was a silly, simple European woman, and they tittered. It was hard for Jackie to bear; she felt the shame of being pointed out publicly and laughed at. But she remembered Christ's sacrifice and how he had been criticised for publicly associating with so-called bad people.

As she left the court one day, a boy being led into the dock signalled wildly to her and called out. He looked frantic. His name was Crazy-boy Chuen; he was an unattractive youngster, sweaty and shaking, his eyes red and runny. He was obviously going through drug withdrawal. He yelled 'Help! I've been framed'. Although she knew nothing about him and had no right to speak, Jackie felt impelled to approach the magistrate.

'Your Honour, I think it possible this boy does not have legal aid. Could you remand the case so that enquiries may be made?'

To her surprise, the magistrate agreed. Jackie and Crazy-boy went to the cell, where she was allowed two minutes to speak with him.

'Listen to me' said Jackie. 'I have no time now to tell you about Jesus. But if you call on His Name, He will hear you. He is God.'

At once, to the astonishment of the prison guard, Crazy-boy did as he was bid and his condition immediately altered. The twitching ceased and his face grew calm.

Next day he was found guilty of attempting to break into cars and was sentenced. Jackie was now convinced that this was untrue. Deciding it was a proper use of money, she hired a lawyer and set about looking for real evidence. Finally she established an unbreakable alibi for Crazy-boy. At the time of the so-called crime he had been watching a movie in Wanchai, several miles away from the car park. This she was able to prove.

Once more Jackie hired a lawyer – expense money always seemed to come when really needed – and a new trial was arranged. The police were annoyed that Jackie was taking up their time in this way over a 'no-good' boy. In spite of past crimes, Jackie believed his innocence of this one. At the end of the trial, Crazy-boy was acquitted and set free. He was not only free – he was a different boy altogether; he had learned from experience that Jesus is alive and active.

Jackie became well-known in the court. David, a young solicitor, began to give his services free to help the boys, provided they told the truth. A legal first occurred when two boys were arrested for apparently claiming to be Triad members, which was unlawful. The boys had signed confessions but later stated that they did this under duress. David was able to produce witnesses to state emphatically that these boys had publicly renounced membership of the Triads on becoming young Christians.

The Judge, for whom hearing about conversions and baptisms was a novel experience, was impressed. 'I see no reason' he said, 'why a man should be branded for life if he wants to change and become a Christian.' The boys were free to go home.

The Judge turned to Jackie, smiling, and said 'It is now your responsibility, Miss Pullinger, to see that the boys do follow the new life they have acknowledged.'

Here was a victory, a recognition that former Triad members could free themselves from the clutches of the gangs and could be recognised as upstanding Christians by the community.

The court appearances were a strain on Jackie and never anything to be welcomed, but she really believed that much Christian witness was seen at these times.

She knew she had made many mistakes in the handling of the boys, but by trial and error, by Christian love and by constant prayer, she went on in faith, encouraged.

She was so delighted when the boys reformed that she was anxious to draw them into the life of the church. But church people found it hard to accept them – the Walled City boys made them uncomfortable. One Sunday the boys burst into church rather late and looking ghastly – they had obviously been in a fight. They afterwards explained that on their way to church they had been attacked by Triad youths. But it was no good trying to put this to the church members, who just could not cope. To them, Jackie's boys were bad lads who should not be tolerated in church and who gave the church a bad name.

Jackie was despondent. 'Surely they should all fit in here like a family,' she thought. A wise, older visiting missionary, George Williamson, came to her rescue. He spoke from long experience.

'Don't make the boys come to church here yet, Jackie' he pleaded. 'They are just not ready for it yet. They're like seedlings – too young yet to transplant.'

'What shall I do then?' asked Jackie, bewildered.

'Look after them yourself in your own prayer fellowship,' said George. 'Then they'll grown strong enough to take the knocks and in time church members will grow up and learn to accept them. It will be better for all.'

Jackie nodded thoughtfully. He could be right! She was being over-anxious. So she gathered the lads into her Bible study group in the club room, a familiar place, and despite mistakes and failures, a deep Christian bond was forged. The treasures of the Christian faith were opened up to the boys in their own language and in terms they could understand. Jackie was much helped by Dora Lee, a splendid Chinese friend who had been head girl at St Stephen's School. She came to assist Jackie. It was she who taught Jackie so much about how Chinese people think and feel and about their age-old culture.

Trial and error was a hard path, but Jackie was making headway. And God did not leave her without help.

9

People do change!

The most thrilling experience to Jackie was to see people change – leaving a destructive way of life and changing to a new, full-blooded, happy existence in Christ. Head-shaking and saying 'You can't change human nature' means nothing to Jackie. She has seen it happen hundreds of times and it is this that makes everything worthwhile for her – the long sleepless hours of service, the gruelling schedules, the disappointments in human relationships, the grim surroundings and evil forces among which she serves.

One night she was sitting in the house in Lung Kong Road feeling really rotten, getting over a dose of 'flu. She had hoped no-one would call that evening but a banging on the door presaged the appearance of Geui Jai, not the most welcome visitor. He was a faded fighter, once a renowned kung-fu expert and one of the few Walled City brothers who had received a reasonable education. He spoke good English and had a style about him.

Yet it was obvious he was on the way down, useless to his Triad boss because of drug dependency. Jackie often came upon him sleeping rough in the street or on a staircase; he had been kicked out of his family home. He injected himself and was a wreck of a young human being.

Tonight he was all smiles and earnestness. 'Please can I borrow your typewriter, Miss Poon' he enquired politely. It seemed that he had to help someone with a Chinese translation and wanted to write a letter.

Bells should have rung in Jackie's head but she was not feeling one hundred per cent. Weakly she agreed to lend it for one evening. Later that night he rang with a rambling tale, asking to keep the typewriter for a few more days.

Jackie now realised she had been taken for a ride. Very probably she would never see the machine again; obviously Geui Jai had pawned it, no doubt for money to buy drugs. She sighed.

She was not the first person to be made a fool of and what she had lost was only a machine after all, but all the same, she was annoyed. Her crossness was nothing to that of her boys. The Lung Kong Road 'family' were really mad at Geui and wanted to beat him up. Jackie persuaded them that this would be no help.

Time passed and she forgot about the typewriter. About three months later, to her surprise, she found the machine had re-appeared in her flat. How did it get there? She asked around and at last one of the lads admitted that the 14K boss Goko was the reason. He had sent for Geui Jai and ordered him to hand over the pawn ticket. He, Goko, had then gone down to the pawnshop and himself paid to recover the machine. He had then caused it to be sent back to Jackie, without any message.

When Jackie learned of this, she sent a strong invitation to Goko to meet her in a tea-shop. To her surprise, the Triad boss agreed and turned up, suavely dressed as usual, a powerful force.

'What a strange character,' thought Jackie. 'On one hand he runs illegal and immoral rackets that he knows I hate, and on the other he goes out of his way to protect a missionary.'

Goko shrugged his shoulders and puffed furiously at his cigarette. He looked embarrassed when Jackie told him how touched she was by his action. 'It was nothing, nothing,' he muttered.

'You redeemed my typewriter, yet I am not your friend or sister – I hate all you do,' said Jackie. Then God gave her the words to speak gently but firmly to Goko of the Saviour, Jesus Christ, and of how He redeemed us with His own blood, buying back our lives while we were still enemies.

'I'm lonely and afraid' said Goko at last.

Despite his awful life-style there were things that were admirable about him. He confessed to Jackie that he admired his own brother Sai Di for following Jesus and he admired the Christians and would want to be a true one if he did surrender.

'But,' he pointed out, 'Christians do not earn much. I have to get together huge sums of money to support my dependants and my brothers – and to do this I am forced to cheat and steal and lie and run rackets.'

Jackie shook her head. Once more, she spoke quietly to him of the forgiving, enabling power of Jesus and the new life that would follow, with answers to many problems. Then she went away – Goko had to make his own decision, like all of us.

He paid the tea-shop bill and hurried off. But he had heard the story of redemption.

It was to be several years before Goko resolved the struggle with himself. But in 1983, Goko, leader of the 14K Triad made his commitment and gave his life to Christ. He was baptised and received a new, Christian name – 'New Paul'. Goko had finally gone.

Much more quickly, good came from the tale of the typewriter. Geui Jai was thoroughly shaken by what had happened and his conscience pricked him. He was fed up with his aimless life, wandering about and sleeping rough; especially when he saw before him the new life of the Lung Kong Road lads. He himself now desired to become a new person. He entered a centre for drug rehabilitation run by a Christian pastor and gave up his syringe. He too had changed.

*　　*　　*　　*　　*　　*

When a family notices changes, it really is impressive. A tough nut to alter was Ah Kei, who considered himself 'an emperor among gang leaders'. He was no foolish boy but a mature man controlling hundreds of 'sai los', with a vice kingdom that stretched far beyond the Walled City. He was admired and feared.

Jackie met him after a whole group of young Triad boys had given their lives to Christ. As usual, Jackie enquired who their 'daih lo' was. Who was their 'big brother'? He was the one who had to be told that he no longer had power over the young brothers.

It seemed that Ah Kei was far too important to concern himself with her, a mere girl, but she persisted and eventually a meeting was arranged in Chaiwan, an enormous crowded area at one end of Hong Kong Island, where thousands of people are rehoused by the Government. Here and in other places Ah Kei had a profitable empire covering prostitution, vice, drug and gambling dens. He was a great show-off.

When they met he said mockingly, 'If you can convert me, Poon Siu Jeh, I'll give you a thousand disciples.' He banged his black leather gloves against his hands and smirked.

'I can't convert you' said Jackie briskly, 'or any of your sai los; these decisions have to be made personally.'

Ah Kei invited Jackie to an expensive meal in a cafe, throwing money about like confetti, all to impress. Suddenly he asked her: 'Poon Siu Jeh, do you look down on drug addicts?'

Jackie shook her head. 'I can't do that; they are people Jesus came into the world for.'

'Would you be friends with one?' asked Ah Kei urgently.

Jackie smiled. 'I am often criticised' she said, 'for having more friends among addicts than among good-living people.'

Ah Kei thought a bit. Then he invited Jackie to go on a tour of his 'vice kingdom'. She realised she was in for a long night. Afterwards she thought it all seemed like a weird dream. During that night she was given the opportunity to speak about Jesus on an amazing journey into vice. In several gambling houses, in one awful drug den, where the 'clients' were thin like stick insects, she was heard with an incredible respect when Ah Kei introduced her as a Christian lady who would not look down on them.

In one den a man with stomach cramp begged for help. All Europeans were thought to have power and money and medical skills. Jackie shook her head at this idea but agreed to pray for the man, providing there was no giggling or disorder. 'I'm going to pray to the living God' she said firmly.

There was silence. Jackie laid her hands on the sick man and prayed for him in the name of Jesus. To everyone's surprise, his whole posture relaxed, he said his pains had left him. He began to ask about this Living God.

After that night, Jackie gave Ah Kei a Bible, prayed with him and for him and 'phoned friends to remember him in their prayers. For several months he was held in the foremost of many thoughts. Ah Kei was really trying to begin a new life. He went home to his neglected wife and children. He relinquished much of his illegal and wicked empire; coming off drugs he was finding much harder. He was still a very proud person, not too sorry about his past and still not conquering his drug habit.

Jackie was disappointed. Jean and Rick Willans were annoyed – they made no bones about it. How could he say he was now a Christian and still not have kicked the drug habit?

Ah Kei himself got dispirited, to the point of saying that Jackie had better give up trying to help him. He became cold and bitter towards her. 'Now I've given up the girls and the dens' he said, 'I've got no money for drugs.' He decided to plan a robbery and forced his wife to get hoods ready and steal a car. But everything went wrong with his foolish plan and nothing happened.

Jean and Rick invited Ah Kei to a party. Whilst in their flat, a prayer group met and during this time, when people were praying in their special heavenly language, something happened to Ah Kei. He suddenly fell forward on his knees with a terrible thump. Apparently he was suddenly overcome by the thought of the rotten life he had lived and the misery he had caused to others. For the first time, he really felt a sense of being a sinful person and he felt genuinely humble and repentant. He himself began to pray.

It was an amazing sight to Jackie – a former Triad boss on his knees. In the Chinese culture, this is the most servile position, especially for a gang leader.

Jean and Rick offered to take Ah Kei into their home and in this prayerful, happy setting, his deliverance from drugs was finally accomplished. This did not occur through Government clinics nor even private doctors, but through the loving prayers of this household. Ah Kei finally threw his drug packets down the lavatory and began to pray in sincerity. Each time the pains came, he prayed and they went away. After three days he was cured.

His old life was now completely behind him. He started honest work in an office. He began to tell other people about the love and power of Jesus. He told not only his family but even the cynical security and customs men at the Chinese border. In his family village in China he was able to explain scriptural passages to a Christian Chinese girl who did not own a Bible. Ah Kei gave his as a gift to her and the word spread.

Jackie was right in a feeling she had had, months before, that the appearance of Ah Kei in her life and his conversion, were to have important results in the Christian circles of Hong Kong.

Ah Kei's wife, Bing, and their children, were naturally very happy too. And Bing's father, who had once despaired of his son-in-law, put his thoughts into a sentence with which no one could argue.

He said: 'I was a young man and now I am an old man, but I have never before seen a bad man become a good man.'

He had never before seen what the power of Jesus can do.

10

Girls, women, mothers and grannies

Her own tomboy days made it easy for Jackie to relate to the young boys of the Walled City. Her distinctive European femininity was used by God in her approaches to the difficult and hardened young men. They reacted to Jackie's charm as well as to her words and deeds. She confessed that it was always easier to help the boys than the girls of the City. The boys had sunk low and knew it. The girls often had little sense of doing wrong; there was so little likelihood of a bright or sweet future for them.

Chinese family life in the Walled City was often founded more on economic prudence than on affection. Families were often large, so that in old age, parents could count on their children to support them. Young Chinese adults often got into debt trying to do this; it was very worrying. Girls in the Walled City were often expected to stop studying and quickly take on paid work. Ah Lin, sister of Christopher of the Youth Club, was expected to look after the babies and carry water and assemble plastic items. Not surprisingly, this endless drudgery led her to run away from home and soon get into trouble.

When Jackie had first gone to the Walled City she had been upset at the sight of the young girls, often little more than children, thin and pretty, who lived immoral lives under the 'protection' of Triad bosses. These girls, selling their bodies and often with little love in their lives, were forced to turn over their takings to their bosses. They were guarded by older women, known as 'mama-sans', and if they tried to run away from their miserable lives, they were usually caught and beaten. Their immoral lives of prostitution as it is called, went on quite publicly and Jackie never forgot the first such sad little girl she saw, squatting in a narrow street by a sewer tunnel. She was undernourished and pathetic, in spite of her lipstick and nail varnish and bold clothes.

Trying to talk to these girls was very difficult. If Jackie approached them, they cringed away. They were embarrassed at having a respectable European lady talking to them.

Some, as they saw it, set their sights a little higher and became ballroom girls. Then, at least, you got better food and some pretty clothes to wear, though these all had to be paid for. Maria was such a girl, forced from home by a step-mother who had wanted her to work on the streets.

Maria's story was sad and no-one knows if it had a happy ending, for she disappeared from Jackie's life. But her story involved Jackie in a sacrifice of something she really treasured. Maria got into debt to a 'loan shark', a ruthless character from whom she had borrowed a large sum of money which she could not repay. This man then demanded that she become his 'snake', his personal property as a prostitute for two years, to pay off her debts. This really terrified Maria – this would indeed be the last straw. She ran to Jackie. Could anything be done?

How could Jackie find 1500 Hong Kong dollars to repay the loan? She had then only about fifteen dollars of her own. But she felt she must break the terrible spiral of events in which Maria was caught. There was only one thing to be done. Jackie must sell her beautiful and expensive oboe, the musical instrument she played in the Hong Kong orchestra.

This was a real wrench, but Jackie thought: 'If Jesus gave up His life, surely I can give up an oboe.'

The money thus raised saved Maria from an awful fate, but there was no certainty that she would not get into more trouble. That was the cynical view of the money-lender, even as he grabbed the dollars that repaid his loan.

A happier story was that of Angel, another desperate girl who, on the run from the Triads, came to seek refuge with Jackie. Passed like a parcel to a bad man, when young, Angel found herself supporting five young men by her immoral earnings. She had tried before to run away but had been captured and beaten. Now she had tried again and had nowhere to go. A thin girl with many bruises, she just had to be helped. Jackie knew they would have to trade with Angel's Triad boy-friend or else she would never be free. It was necessary to hold a 'gong-sou' or talk-out and decide on a separation fee, to get Angel away from the gang. This turned out to be a difficult and dangerous business, with Jackie and Angel facing a bunch of Triad hoodlums and with more of these outside the cafe with weapons. Angel had lost all her spirit and could not resist anyone and Jackie was frightened by the fierce, uncouth men who confronted her. She knew things could get bad, especially if 'her' Walled City boys – who were watching nearby – came out to defend her. There could then be bloodshed indeed. Jackie said some quick urgent prayers. At last, by a hurried phone call from the cafe, Jackie summoned friends and the police, who captured several of the gangsters who were clutching iron bars, and who were waiting on the doorstep of Angel's home.

Angel was free at last. It was not easy for her – people did not easily forget a girl's past – there was no glory attached to that. But Angel was found somewhere to live with good, friendly people and, though she had never been to school in her life, she began to learn to read. She was never molested again. Later she married a young Chinese Christian with a steady job and a totally new life opened for her. She ws one of the more blessed ones.

* * * * * *

Mothers often had hard lives in the Walled City. Many had husbands in crime – on drugs or without regular jobs. These women had to work in their dingy homes, sometimes assembling plastic objects, or sewing on sequins. There was little respect between husband and wife and the rest of the family. Mrs Chung, a tiny thirty-year old with five children, had a drug-addicted husband who brought in little money. They and the five children lived on top of a double bed; the space it stood on was merely the roof of someone's shack. On this bed they slept, cooked, played and worked.

Little Mrs Chung carried water buckets for a living, despite her bad legs. She heard the story of Jesus through the Youth Club boys and became a vivd Christian, smiling despite her dismal existence. Jackie managed to get a little financial help for the family but it was not sufficient. Then an awful cough settled on Mrs Chung and she died from tuberculosis. The life of the children with their father proved unbearable and they soon ran away and turned up at Jackie's house. Jackie did not think her premises were very suitable but she could not turn away a pathetic battered thirteen-year old girl and a baby, so in they came and stayed. The youngsters were at first very silent and it was a long time before they could mix and chatter as children should. The Lung Kong Road boys were good at playing with the baby and he soon became part of the family.

*   *   *   *   *   *

When Jackie had first visited the Walled City and played the harmonium for Auntie Donnithorne, she had met many grannies, many of them not nearly so old as they looked. They shuffled along in their Chinese slippers, in their black trouser suits and smiled, creasing their lined brown faces. As well as caring for tiny grandchildren, older Chinese women still work hard in the colony today and can be seen working on building sites or, out in the rural New Territories, carrying great piles of hay or vegetables in tubs fastened to yokes across the shoulders. These old ladies look frail but are incredibly tough.

Some Jackie met were not nice old ladies. They had led lives of crime and immorality. Some thought she was simple and traded on this. One old granny, brought along by a grandson, looked pathetic and had a badly gashed wound on her head, visible through a dirty bandage.

'I want to be baptised' she murmured. Jackie's instinct told her not to believe this. She soon ferreted

70

out the truth which was that the old lady, having fallen down and given herself a mighty bang on the head, thought she might die and was afraid to do so without a burial spot. These plots cost a lot of money. The old lady knew that if she had a certificate saying she was a member of the Christian church, she could get a piece of land at a reasonable price. This is what she was after.

Jackie saw through this ploy but took her to join some other grannies, who talked to her tenderly and led her to understand what baptism was all about. Later the old woman did give her life to Christ and was baptised. She died not long after and did have her burial plot.

One lovely lady, who had known no real joy and had never heard of Jesus, came into Jackie's life and found peace and healing in a meeting for prayer. Hands were laid on her and her breathing difficulties ceased.

This little lady became quite radiant and delighted in making herself useful in the Lung Kong house. She cleaned, cooked, and brought her friends from the street market, who sold provisions cheaply to the residents. She was so thrilled with her new life, at peace from her vicious criminal son, that she declared Jackie to be her 'kai neui' – her god-daughter – and to Jackie she became 'kai ma' – godmother. Since Jackie was so far away from her own much loved mother, this new simple relationship was tender and touching.

Girls, women, mothers, grannies – who knew who might not turn up for help? It thrilled Jackie when she and her team of friends and helpers were really able to do something practical and above all to bring the love of Jesus to lonely, outcast, suffering girls and women.

11

Safe houses

'You will make a good worker, Miss Poon, because you care.' So said Pastor Chan, who had opened a farm out in the rural New Territories, to help drug addicts come through withdrawal. Jackie admired him, since he ploughed a lone furrow in claiming to bring junkies off drugs without the usual medical help. Here at the farm, residents began a new life and stayed there for about eighteen months of loving care. Since Jackie was so impressed by what the pastor was doing, she appreciated his encouraging words about her own ministry.

Social workers in Government agencies also worked in drug centres but they were taught not to get involved with their cases, but to keep their feelings at bay. Jackie did not believe she could work like that – she needed to feel personally for individual junkies. Indeed, without caring so much about them, she did not think she could put up with the unpleasantness and the pain of dealing with them. Only the power of God within her, she believed, enabled her to carry on.

Pressures were convincing Jackie that she and her own helpers needed somewhere like the Chan farm – some separate place where people who truly desired to get off drugs and start a new Christian life could stay for a while. It needed time to accustom them to a new stable way of life, for most of them had grown up to lying, stealing, cheating as part of everyday life.

She did not want such people at Lung Kong Road. It was not fair or helpful to the boys already cured who lodged there. Also, if they lived at Lung Kong, addicts could soon obtain secret supplies of drugs in the Walled City nearby, if they relapsed.

What was to be done? Things were getting desperate. Ah Kei, so dramatically changed from being a Triad gang leader, was very worried about a relative, Ah Kit. Ah Kit had come off drugs and was one of the lucky ones to be housed with Jean and Rick Willans. But he had begun to take over their lives, demanding constant attention and affection; it was all too much and the Willans's daughter had threatened to leave home. Somewhere had to be found.

An answer came in the miraculous sort of way Jackie was now getting used to. While she was visiting her parents in England, exciting news reached her. Jean Willans had written a lively book on her religious experiences and an appreciative reader had sent money to Hong Kong for precisely the purpose of founding a home for drug addicts. A miracle indeed, this was compounded when a new flat became easily available and became known as the House of Stephen. This title, the Society of Stephen, was registered for legal purposes to cover the work done by Jackie and the Willans family on behalf of junkies. Life in the new flat began with four boys sleeping on the floor.

It was hard to refuse permission to people eager for a new life and soon prayers were said for another dwelling. An English friend came up with the necessary cash and a further home was opened.

People were never persuaded to come to these 'safe houses' against their will, nor unless they truly wanted to begin a completely new life; they knew that if they did come, they would have to stay for the required length of time. Jackie had learned that if they hurried away directly after a cure, they would probably soon be back.

Many of the men who now clamoured to be admitted came from parts of Hong Kong outside the Walled City. Some came through meeting friends already cured. Lots of the new junkies arriving knew nothing at all about Jesus Christ. There was so much to pass on.

Jackie believed that these people's new faith did not depend upon their understanding doctrine but upon seeing the power of Jesus working in others' lives and then in their own lives. Simple prayers were answered and simple faith expanded and grew. It was not 'mind over matter' explained Jackie to doubting enquirers – most of the junkies, until cured, had little thinking ability – their minds were half dead. After they had obtained the marvellous benefits of praying in the Spirit and of being cured, they were likely to come to a true understanding of the Saviour, his Cross, forgiveness and redemption.

For years Jackie had tried frantically to do all the jobs herself. Now she was involved with many helpers and began to see the meaning of 'the body of Christ' as a group of people working together, each with their own function. It was very thrilling.

The routine in the Stephen Houses was steady but not dull. As well as prayers and Bible study, the residents were given coaching in Chinese and

English. They also took on jobs in the household which they enjoyed when doing them all together.

Football was a great way of letting off steam. As the pitch was next door to the Government centre for drug cure, it was interesting to see people from the centre hanging about by the football pitch, clearly impressed by the strong healthy lads playing there who were once totally zapped out on heroin. They were a good advertisement for the Stephen Houses.

*   *   *   *   *   *

Somebody gave the house a rotary floor polisher that would cover big areas and was in good working order. This gave Jackie the idea of hiring out teams of boys who would go to the island and wax and polish parquet floors. Keen, smart operators, they made a big impression. They were supervised by Tony, by birth a Cuban, who in spotless white, watched over the teams with mlitary efficiency.

Tony was used to the exercise of power, but in a very different way. After an unsettled childhood, he had entered Hong Kong as a refugee and was soon picked up by the Triads and initiated into a life of crime, including robbery with violence. At sixteen he began to take heroin. He had no one to care for him and felt that no one did or could. Yet he was feared as the leader of a new Triad branch of the 14K and was involved in fights, blackmail and murder. He had to fight to maintain supremacy. The various awful strains upon him caused a personality collapse. When Jackie was called to him, he was sitting as in a trance, resigned to dying. He tried to give away to Jackie the land on which his house was, but she refused to listen to this.

'We don't want your land, we want you!' she cried.

'Come with me' she urged, trying to get him into the waiting taxi. He shook his head and kept muttering 'no good, no good'. But Jackie persisted. Dimly he heard the words she kept repeating – 'God has chosen you. He has chosen to save you. He wants you. Come with us.' She went on and on.

Hardly believing he would respond, she climbed slowly into the taxi, her heart sinking. To her amazement, Tony tottered to his feet and staggered to the taxi, climbed in and sank down beside her. It was the last he was to see of his gang village.

The boys welcomed him at Lung Kong Road and in their own way led him into a true relationship with the Living Lord. A long time later he wrote down his own testimony, one of many, saying how at that time he had cried like a little child – this proud gang leader. He knew he had been truly 'born again'.

In time, Tony trained as a hair stylist and went to live with the Willans family, Jean and Rick becoming his spiritual parents. In such wonderful ways were his deep needs met.

Older men began to appear, begging admission. Jackie was not keen at first, thinking they would not mix well with the younger lads from the Walled City. She wondered if she could control them. Some of the men had long lives of crime and addiction behind them and were hard cases. Back came the first two who would not take no for an answer. Finally she relented and took them in. To her surprise they fitted in well and made a more balanced family.

'God was adding fathers to us as well' she smiled.

Many practical issues, such as dental treatment, arose, for heroin addiction rots the teeth terribly. Fortunately, the British army came to their rescue and severe cases were treated at the military hospital. The army also gave them empty camp sites and helped with coaches for outings. God worked in so many marvellous and mysterious ways, Jackie decided.

In the first twenty months at St Stephen's, seventy-five boys were taken in and every one came off heroin without pain or trial, by praying in tongues, by the touch of Jesus, and by the loving care they received. As Jackie said, 'these were heady days.'

12

Strange parishes

In Mongkok, an area of Hong Kong said by some to be 'the most crowded place on earth', forty older men live in wire cages. They and their total possessions are contained in a series of two-tiered wire mesh cubicles in a tenement. These cage tenements are cramped, depressing and a fire risk. And the caged men are lonely, helpless and fatalistic. But they have no proper homes and have chosen to live like this, rather than out on the streets.

About fourteen hundred Hong Kong people are thought to live and sleep rough on the streets to this day. While they are not likely often to feel cold, and seem to manage to get some food, it is not a lifestyle that any people or government can be proud of.

When Jackie first visited the Walled City she fell over people sleeping rough, on staircases, by the side of the path, on landings and roofs. But all over the territory you can find people at night bedding down on the pavements and in alleyways.

Jackie was filled with a great compassion towards these homeless people and she thought of Jesus, the one who understood them utterly, the one who in his earthly life had 'no place to lay his head.' She and her team would try to give some help where they could.

Some of the street-sleepers had simply lost heart. One of the team would chat with them and try to encourage them to a new dignity. Attempts would be made to get the people housed by government, and in the meantime to obtain blankets and clothing. They made appointments with the social welfare agencies and saw that the street people actually kept these.

Sometimes the team would see really ill people lying groaning within a few feet of passing tourists; they would contact medical services and try to arrange for treatment. It was a never-ending task but each person given a new chance of better living made the team happy.

Jackie found one man who had slept on the streets for thirty years. He was a horrible sight, seldom washed, slimy and distinctly unappealing. He did have some family and a well-set-up brother who would have nothing to do with him. It was hardly surprising. Apparently the brother, a rather self-righteous man, had sent a Bible to the street-dweller, which was fairly useless since he could not read. Jackie was determined that the luckier brother should take more responsibility and that the street man should make a new effort. She contrived a meeting in a smart tea-house where a kind of getting together was effected.

It rather amused Jackie to take the street people for a real slap-up meal in a high-class tea shop and see the strange looks of the other customers.

So many bad situations have to be fought and overcome in Hong Kong. Jackie felt that God was constantly reminding them of the need to be flexible and mobile in the fight against evil. They must be prepared to go anywhere, however strange their 'parish', to achieve victory. It was a sort of guerilla war! Where would it take them next?

Another unusual parish involved Jackie and her friends in the lives of refugees. When you think that there are probably over five million people in Hong Kong, it is hard to recall that when it was ceded to the British in 1842, Lord Palmerston, then Prime Minister, called it 'a barren island with hardly a house on it'. It has since become not only a prosperous money centre, but a haven for refugees.

Refugees have proved a big problem for government. In 1949, the first wave of homeless people arrived in the colony from China, after Communist forces took over the Chinese government. When the Vietnam war ended in 1975, Vietnamese refugees, known to most of us as 'boat people', began to flood in. They endured terrible journeys to reach safety and freedom. How to house all these people has continued to be a vast worry.

There are still thousands of boat people in open and closed camps waiting to be resettled in some other countries and start a new life. Unfortunately, many countries are not eager to take them. They are therefore forced to live a very restricted life in their iron dwellings, with little privacy. It is hard for them to keep up hope.

Many refugees are housed on outlying islands but in 1979, when the drug problems seemed a little less urgent, Jackie and some of her young team began to spend time at a camp called Tuen Mun, outside Kowloon. This housed over one thousand boat people, sleeping two hundred to a section, with no more space than room to put a sleeping mat on the floor. It was just a little better than sleeping in the street.

Jackie assisted a missionary doctor, Doctor Dale, and also held classes to teach English, and ran Bible classes. The situation of the refugees permitted no sentiment. It was no good pretending that very quickly you would all be flown to America, the idea of many boat people. But Jackie and her team offered the same loving Christ of whom they had spoken to the junkies.

There was also practical work to be done, simple things to prepare for the hoped-for day of departure to a western country. There was need to learn how to brush teeth, use a knife in the European way, simple basic things to us but not to oriental people used to different life-styles.

Jackie's third strange parish led her into Hong Kong's prisons. Her work in the magistrates' courts sometimes meant that she saw young men sentenced and committed to Stanley prison. Since she cared about them, she could not leave matters there and frequently asked permission to visit. She was not there to speak of their cases, but to give pastoral help and remind them of the continuing, forgiving love of Jesus.

Here she moved among hardened villains, men who had committed robbery, rape, even murder, yet there were life-changes resulting from her visits. The awful sense of their own hopelessness often led the prisoners to want to change their ways.

Jackie was not stupid and was by now experienced in dealing with villains. She knew the difference between 'hauh-fui' (regret) and 'fui-goih' (repent). Many prisoners did regret what they had done, because it had landed them in so much trouble.

When they were really inwardly sorry, Jackie

could lead them on to the discovery of the power of Jesus to change their hearts and give a new peace.

She talked to one young man, nineteen, who was in prison for a serious assault. He had been impressed by the change of another prisoner from bitterness and hatred to softness of heart and compassion. He asked how this could be brought about. Jackie was delighted once again to talk of Jesus. At first the youth was nervous and uncomfortable but gradually relaxed and seemed to understand.

At the end of the interview, he accepted that Jesus was the Son of the true God and could save him; he cried that he would follow Him. Then came the crunch. His solicitor had told him to plead 'not guilty'. But he turned to Jackie and said, sadly but firmly, 'But I am guilty and I must say so.' This he did and was sentenced to nine years. In prison Jackie went on seeing him and he did not stop believing.

Sometimes, visits seemed disappointing but paid off in the end. So it was with Daih So, to whom Jackie spoke in the bleak general visiting hall, where she could talk only through a wire mesh and a pane of glass. He was thirty, but as he had been on drugs for years, he looked much older. He knew what sin was all right – 'It's walking your own way,' he said. He seemed not to heed Jackie, was more intent on his next 'fix' and called the guard to take him away.

Jackie was sad as she left. Yet six months later, she was approached in the street by a plump, bright man who turned out to be Daih So. He was coming to tell her that her sad face as he had left the prison cell had so touched him that he had, then and there, decided to let Jesus into his heart. He had since come off drugs and kept on praying in Jesus's name. Jackie was overjoyed.

Sometimes the team had to direct people towards jail rather than otherwise. This happened with Ah Wah who had been living a changed life since going to a Stephen House. Now he felt he must confess to the police an outstanding court case which he had evaded by jumping bail. Now that he was a new person, he felt he had to put this right; his conscience was troubling him.

Jackie had to agree with him. For various reasons, it was quite hard getting him arrested! The taxi did not come, a car would not start. Finally they reached the police station and the police seemed not keen to do anything and could not find his papers. At last they went before the magistrate and Ah Wah explained about his new life and his guilty conscience. The magistrate was sympathetic.

'Congratulations,' he said, 'you did the right thing. I wish you every blessing in your new life; you can go.'

Sometimes the prisoners themselves made Jackie feel humble. Kwok, who had narrowly excaped execution and was in prison for life, presented Jackie with a list of long-term prisoners who 'needed praying for'. Jackie herself and her team knew that they received the prayers of prisoners for them.

'Don't worry about us' said Kwok one day when Jackie visited; she was a little tired and down. 'We're all right here,' said Kwok, 'and we're praying for you.'

There were strange parishes as well as the Walled City but God was working in all of them.

13

Out in the sunshine

Jackie seemed to be giving most of her life to the Walled City, touring its tunnelled gloom, but sometimes she emerged into the sunshine. The brilliant beating sun is a feature of Hong Kong, sun that is delightful if you are swimming in the warm sea or lazing on the splendid beaches, but merciless to those who have no air-conditioning.

Once in a while she would take the rack railway tram up to 'the Peak', a height on Hong Kong Island from which you get glorious views of the sparkling bay and the surrounding islands, and where you are bound to be joined by cheerful chattering Chinese families.

Sometimes she would find herself walking in the crowded tourist and business districts, where the tall skyscrapers, their windows winking in the strong light, remind you of New York. Visitors and government residents are enjoying life, hailing taxis, purchasing silk, jade, scrolls, basket ware, and ordering meals – spending, spending, spending. Money is in the very air of Hong Kong and has been from its earliest trading days.

Outside the stock exchange, ordinary Chinese people stand gazing up at the share index, prominently displayed outside the building. Have they made money? Are their investments doing well?

Jackie's insights soon penetrated beneath the surface of the dynamic, thrusting life of the colony. She saw the desperate human and spiritual need inseparable from the lure of wealth.

In a colony with modest provision for social services and pensions, getting, making and keeping jobs is important. Poorer people, with little to offer an employee, must work hard. Many do so splendidly in the catering industry, but the hours are long and wearying.

Mothers must work in factories and this brings problems; not so easy there to see to their baby. 'The baby is my responsibility' says Grannie, who accepts this as part of life. Or else, the responsibility of smaller children. So Jackie saw dozens of little five-year-olds, girls, each with a baby strapped to her back, neither very clean, taking a share in the family economy.

For older children, those lucky enough to get some education, there is the problem of privacy. How can you do homework properly in a crowded family shack with never a minute to yourself, babies crying and toddlers jumping about? Jackie often walked into a bank or museum or other public building and saw shining heads bent over tables, or sitting studying on the corner of a public bench. School-children in immaculate white doing home-work in a cool, marble-floored building, anywhere in fact with air-conditioning where they would be left in peace. Preparation for good solid jobs does not come easily. Jackie came to know that some young people cannot take the competition and the worrying strain and jump off buildings. It made her heart heavy.

The fight for life and the shortage of living room does not make things easy. Jackie visited one of the famous ladder streets, lanes made up of rising steps, similar to many in Paris. Alongside these are little stalls selling gew-gaws and costume jewellery. In one of these she saw an old bent man, a vegetable seller. He lived in a cupboard, a few feet square. Here he stored his vegetables, bringing them out each morning to display. Late at night, when no more customers will buy, he put the goods back into his cupboard and climbed in himself. 'I sleep on top here' he said with a shrug – he has no other home.

At least he has a regular pitch for work. Some women earn their living ironing shirts on an ironing-board in the midst of a market street, with electricity tapped from the overhead wires. When they have finished the great pile of shirts, they fold up the board, disconnect the iron and drag the whole outfit, shirts and all, back to their homes. Another man runs a business from a plastic bag, selling things by the roadside. At least no one will move him on.

It is the contrasts in the colony that are so startling; the life of the working Cantonese people is so starkly different from that of those who live in gold-fronted houses and drive about in gold automobiles, whether Europeans or 'fat cat' Chinese. Even now Jackie has not got used to these great differences.

* * * * * *

There is much seediness in the entertainment areas of the colony, with its garish night-life, its blue movies, porno palaces and night clubs. Jackie feels compassion for those forced to work in such places and fierce revulsion at those who run them.

Sometimes she goes out into the countryside of the New Territories, that area of Hong Kong which lies between crowded Kowloon and the border of Red China. Here you can often imagine yourself back in the past, despite the growth of new towns like Shatin, with its splendid race-course. Life is still hard for many peasants in the New Territories. Many work in the rice fields and spend their entire lives bent almost double. The water-buffalo is a familiar sight. Hakka women can be seen at work, wearing their traditional straw hats, with huge brims to keep off the sun, a hole in the top and a sort of short black curtain hanging round the edges of the hat keeping sun from the back of the neck. These women often have their babies strapped to their backs and the tiny infants bounce up and down in an alarming way.

Here and there are really old-style Chinese villages, walled all around, where life still goes on in the traditional manner, observing all the Chinese Festivals and working the land. Over everything hangs the sour smell of night soil, with which the New Territories are fertilised. The neat terraces of vegetables, immaculately kept, gleam greenly in the bright light.

At least there is openness, space, in the New Territories. Back in the crowded city, you have to shout to make yourself heard. Walking round the alleyways in the evening, of which Jackie has no fear, she hears the sound of the mahjong tiles as they are slapped down. The tiles, especially when made of ivory, are most beautiful but the gambling habit which underlies this favourite Chinese table game is destructive. Gambling is illegal in Hong Kong, apart from that organised on the race course, but there is nothing to stop you taking the hydrofoil over to Portugese Macau, where in the casino tourists and Chinese gamble their money away. That there is still so much to pray about continues to be clear to Jackie.

At Aberdeen, where the boat people congregate, the unique life-style of these Chinese people is stil evident. Some never go ashore, spending their lives squashed on to their boats, where social workers and destists occasionally thread their way to see what is happening to the children. Should typhoons occur, as they sometimes do in summer, the boat people, even in their typhoon haven, run great risks. Boats are flung about and buildings inland destroyed. All these things the Chinese endure with time-honoured stoicism and they shrug their shoulders and start again. They are great survivors. But Jackie wants more for them than this – a happier, more peaceful, more purposeful existence.

So as she goes about the colony, she prays quietly to herself, for she is sensitive enough to see need everywhere. An acquaintance, a visiting American sailor, teased her about her habit of praying in tongues so frequently.

'That's how God is able to use me' she insists, 'because I keep in touch.' She invited him to spend one whole day with her going round the colony in this spirit of prayer and seeing what opportunities for Christian witness arose. Rather shyly, he agreed. At the end of the day he was completely convinced. He had seen so much through Jackie's eyes and had seen need and Christian response.

He had seen marvellous things happening before

his eyes. In Jordan Road, a squashed up area in Kowloon, he followed Jackie as she marched into a building with an unsavoury reputation, looking for a tramp whose fortunes she had been following for some time. Known as the 'king of the cats', Mau Wong was a 'protector' for various prostitutes, not a poor man. But he was not happy, as he struggled with his conscience. On this occasion, when they finally located him, he confessed to awful stomach pains and was in distress. Praying quietly in their heavenly language, Jackie and the sailor gently laid their hands on his head. Within a few minutes, he had relaxed and said his pains had gone. He then began to pray himself, an extraordinary sight. A few weeks later, when Jackie once more saw him on his iron staircase, she listened with delight to what he had to tell her.

'I am going to follow Jesus' he said. What is more, he had faced the fact that his big income from the vice rackets would have to go, but he seemed unworried.

'I will have to earn a living in an honest way' he said, 'so I've bought some shoe-brushes and am going to be a boot-black . . . American tourists will pay' he added with a grin.

To seal his pact he solemnly handed over to Jackie an alarming-looking knife, with which he had formerly gone about armed; Mau Wong was on the way to becoming a new and better man.

In many such ways, Jackie witnessed out in the sunshine, as well as in the darkness of the Walled City. It was her greatest thrill to bring inner light and warmth into dark, starved lives and to see Jesus at work.

14

Ready for the future

Hong Kong is in a state of turmoil. As it waits to revert to the People's Republic of China in 1997, despite meetings and arrangements and promises, there is an air of unease. People cannot be sure what is going to happen.

Jackie and her friends and helpers are well aware of this. They accept that the only reliable continuity lies in the certainty of the changeless nature of God's love. So they work on, with a heightened sense of urgency and significance.

Jackie admits to the belief that the poor, simple, unlearned, desperate, are tremendously important to God and will form the spearhead of a true religious revival. These people have less pride to deal with, and can more easily be used by God.

However, though her main work is among the deprived and those who have sunk low, not all the victories are among criminals or the dregs of society. An English former public schoolboy witnesses in an educated voice to his new freedom from drugs and to his new start in life. And a big impact on the Hong Kong police has been made by Ted. Scottish Ted, a CID Officer, a huge rugby player and judo champion, met up with Jackie and Jean in the court-room at one of the trials which Jackie ceaselessly attended. After a verdict releasing the prisoner into Jackie's care, Ted came to chat with them, suggesting they all stay to lunch together. He was obviously interested and intrigued by their attitudes. He was excellent company and the lunch ended with an invitation to Ted to come to Saturday evening prayers. Would he come?

He not only came but was deeply affected. He said 'this is the strangest Saturday evening I've ever spent. I'm usually out with the boys, drinking, but tonight I've been really inspired by something I don't understand.' Smiling, Jean gave him a copy of her book to take away.

A little while later, Ted rang Jackie to say that he had been really disturbed by the book. 'You can't get away from the evidence,' he said, 'I've seen for myself how the boys' lives have been changed. All this about Jesus must be true.'

Jean and Jackie were thrilled, but not surprised. The following Sunday, Ted was baptised in the South China Sea, along with a former gang-member and his wife.

Despite the immense population of Hong Kong, news soon gets about, especially among Europeans. Before long, everyone knew about Ted's conversion. Some of his colleagues joked with him but there was a new respect. A new dimension had entered Ted's life.

The normal work of Jackie's teams goes on and intensifies. 'Safe' houses for ex-junkies and those trying to get away from crime have multiplied and are to be found in city camps, island flats and in what Jackie describes as a 'dream house' at Tai Tam, in a garden by the sea. Here, she says, God even supplied a 'roofer' to replace the broken roof. Tai Tam is already bursting at the seams.

There is progressive local outreach. Dickson makes many contacts, Chinese speaking to Chinese. Families are reconciled. Ah Chiu has forgiven the father who had hung him with wire from the ceiling as a boy! They are both baptised; so many signs of what God can do.

More gifts of the Spirit become evident. At the meetings of a special team which came for a seminar, some genuine healings took place. Nothing is impossible.

The street work expands dramatically. Luke has taken over family visits and is building up a team of co-workers with the same vision. They are in contact with over one hundred families, tirelessly tramping round in the humidity.

By now, Jackie is, to outsiders, famous, though she herself would hate this word. She says she is used by God for marvellous things to happen and the publicity has to be suffered and used. So she and her team of witnesses and musicians make several tours each year far beyond the confines of Hong Kong, to tell what God has done and also to undertake practical work in specially needy situations.

Work is starting in Macau. The team has visited New Zealand and the Philippines, as well as Britian. A proposed tour is to South Africa and an invitation has been received for more involvement in ministry in China. Jay took a team to Thailand to help build a central church meeting place for several tribes in the north of the country.

Jackie believes there is a change in the atmosphere of Hong Kong quite apart from the restless political climate. Local churches are asking for teams – they are suddenly thirsty for the results of the Spirit.

In the Walled City, some of the drug and

gambling dens have been closed down. The anti-corruption campaign helped, but many former criminals have turned to Christianity. The police are well aware of the presence of Miss Poon and her helpers. There have been fewer 'pouncings' on street boys if they are known to have connections with 'that European woman'. And it is known that her word is her bond.

Great changes are undoubtedly ahead. Jackie speaks plainly and fearlessly of what might be in store. 'If spiritual persecution should come, we should be found ready' she says.

In the meantime she goes on, taking and making opportunities to bring the life-changing love of Jesus to all and sundry. Says a well-placed European woman who has watched Jackie, seen her at work and attended her meetings: 'The atmosphere of love in her houses is something you can cut with a knife! She is a truly charismatic person – you can feel immense power coming from her.'

Another person tells of a Bible story mime carried out by an American team in which some of Jackie's boys took part. This was held in the Landmark, a huge shopping complex. Up there on the podium where the bands play and sophisticated exhibitions are held, the story of Jesus was unfolded. Crowds gathered to watch. The boys took their parts with earnestness and sensitivity.

'It was so moving' says a witness, 'tears came into my eyes.' 'Yes' acknowledged Jackie, 'and you would feel even more deeply if you knew the history of some of the boys; they are different lads now!'

The Walled City waits to be demolished; soon the bulldozers will move in and the history of this ghastly place will come to an end. Moving everyone out and rehousing them is bound to bring problems, not only of accommodation but also in the bursting into the colony of criminals and degraded citizens, of whom there are still plenty in the Walled City. But plans are being made for a special mission to be held and Jackie talks enthusiastically of the planting of new Chinese churches.

'The work will be done by groups split almost equally between those who have paid jobs and those who work full time on the streets ministering the Gospel.'

Even the big institutions cannot ignore Jackie and her work. The Government has given her abandoned army huts, the army has given her coach facilities and camp sites, the police gave her a walkie-talkie among other things, and a High Court Judge paid for a Christmas dinner for the boys. As one of the young men said to Jackie, years ago; 'You aren't one of those do-gooders who come to look at us, take photographs, write articles and then go away – you mean to stay.'

Jackie Pulllinger came to Hong Kong over twenty years ago. And she stays, still finding ways of saying 'Try Jesus' – 'Yeh sou ngoi' – Jesus loves you!